So Everyone Else Will Know

# So Everyone Else Will Know

Poems by

David Ricchiute

Cover design by Shay Culligan

ISBN: 978-1-949229-42-4

*Kelsay Books*
Aldrich Press
www.kelsaybooks.com

*to Jean*
*for loving me back*

# Acknowledgments

I am grateful to the editors who first took these pieces, some in somewhat different form: Lee Chapman, *First Intensity* ("Their Version", "The Form of a Lifeform"); Erica Dawson, *Tampa Review* ("Alternate Tongue"); John Gill, *North Atlantic Review* ("Beached on White Sheets", "Eyes", "What Have They Told You?"); Sonia Greenfield, *Rise Up Review* ("Treasure"); Rebecca Harbor, *POEM* ("Language Almost Always Means", "Interior"); Barry Harris, *Tipton Poetry Journal* ("A Blind Eye", "Retraction"); Heather Lenore, *East Coast Literary Review* ("If Even At All", "Versions"); Gordon Lish, *The Quarterly* ("From Inside the Jewelry Store Window", "Tablescape"); Julie MacDonald, *Red Rock Review* ("Clothesline", "Transition", "Saltmarsh", "Scrimshaw"); Robert Nazarene, *American Journal of Poetry* ("Contagion"); A. Wilber Stevens, *Interim* ("Fate", "What Strange Things Lurk"); Robin Stratton, *Boston Literary Magazine* ("Margins"); Dianne Williams, *NOON* ("Isn't It Better That She Knows?").

# Contents

III  entirely alive in gesture and speech

IV  a word is especially good to have

V  the alter ego of making do

# I

at once, with a jolt, and for good

.

# Contagion

My conscience demanded I visit the boy,
the neighborhood boy,
the stricken boy in the iron lung.
Still, I can hear the fan-belt motor
and see his head & collared neck,
slightly inclined on a thin white pillow,
eyes calling from a hapless face,
from a mounted mirror, from a wall mirror
serving no purpose at all.
Ever so utterly against my will,
I stood there almost still in the room,
face positioned just right just so
to not ever once even glance at the eyes,
glance at the eyes, glance at the eyes
that followed me.

A child then, I am startled now
to learn that some who led full lives
are stricken again in later life
by regrown nerves that won't quite last
as long as the rest of their body could.
I'd long forgotten the neighborhood boy
till happening upon a middle-aged man
who saw what he didn't see coming twice,
first in a playground, a pool, or a creek
and now in intolerably weakened legs
that presented to him as they had years before,
foretelling a sentence no one imagined
until the accounts began rolling in,
exposing a generation beached in surrender,
tone deaf to the contagion of things,
a body for a tomb.

# Alternate Tongue

In a voice made almost
entirely of breath, she asks
me, *Tell me?* My tongue
touches folds at the tip
of my palate, "o" drags
air from my throat.

If she were in my mouth,
she could say, *Say a vowel,*
to feel the arrangements I
was making, spoken in order
from front to back—*bills,*
*penalties, documents, drives,*
*cash, lockout, nothing in ink.*

This seems somehow a deeper
telling, disguised in an assembly
of acoustics and sound, divined
from me in an alternate tongue.
*No* is tactile, forceful, bold
in a way that *yes* is anything else.

# Transition

Lying alone,
if not by himself,
he edges nearer,
eyelids closed,
to inhale again,
if never before,
the oscillating warmth
of her oncoming breath,
missed altogether
in the everyday,
as anyone misses
anyone's breath,
for all we see
that seems more there
—the identity of a person
beneath bare skin,
the flight to indifference
exclusion brings—

before an awakened sensibility
voices the last few
telltale signs,
revealing the spectacle
of an altered bearing
—a change in posture,
carriage, gait;
fingers trembling
in vague disassembly,
angling forward,
reaching in—
exposing a person
caught up to a body,
fully formed in gesture & speech,
confirming she'd never

be here again
in any way like
she had been before
if ever he thought she were.

# Retraction

She arrives at my room, this grown-up child,
my entry into life for a third time. Porcelain skin,
grey-green eyes, and a fluent gait that centers a room
wherever her next step happens to fall.
We talk—as her mother and I had done—
of things I'd saved in the weeks gone by
but of none of the things I kept to myself:

clues her mother crocheted in verse,
hunched by a table into the night,
tethered to whatever took hold on the page,
so frail from the wounds she thought she carried.
*You're well?* the child asks. *Am now,* I say.
*You're loved*, I say. *Am now,* she says.

*May I ask ...,* she begins—begins to ask—
when *yes* comes out before she can.
*Was there ever the rest of the night
for her?* Her gaze toward the window
holds her still. Who knows if her mother had any rest
from the force of the voices that came at night.

She leaves in a while, a dreaded while,
again in a way that will trouble me again
if I watch from a window, this ethereal child
who, for reasons she may not even know, sinks
her shoulders inside of herself in a subtle
but visibly transformative retraction.

*You know you do that,* I could say next time,
as I said to her all too-silent mother,
who'd brood in a manner so abject and base
that we, both of us, were helpless to speak.
She does or doesn't or can't or won't.
There is no reading between the lines.
There's only children who draw the line.

# Octet with Wind

Wind from a long-
awaited rain
rattles a shutter,
a screen, or a jamb,
depending on the window
gusts bear in on
to accompany pairs
of oboes, bassoons,
clarinets, & horns
arranged to unwind
in a series of movements,
masking variations
of an endless echo,
chanted in a whisper
her voice repeats
—or ever so faintly
strains to repeat—
exciting her wave lines
to narrow & leap,
calling again
for another diversion
as vital to calm
as uplifting wind
to a symphony of aspen trees
that transforms the silence
into water over the damned
as leaves in the air
take wing to expose
an alabaster clear
flexible line
concealed behind
a cathedral screen,
soothing the echoing voice
to sleep.

# Interior

A worn French easel supports an oil
in an aging artist's subsidized room.
Unlike the interiors Matisse painted
*les Fauves*, the barely-furnished
cold-water flat has little in common
with a room by the sea.

No fabric, no vase, no color to speak of.
Only a photo of one young child
lies on the table by a letter and a pen.
Did she say *no* to say *yes* to herself?
Is near truth ever quite near enough?

Having sat as still as the shore would be
if the moon went down for good, she leans
toward the easel, brush in hand, and
struggles to mask where her brush last
caught the absence in the scene. Even
in her art, to herself she lies.

# In Midair, Astray

Who would have guessed
that right there before us

—so far below
where we'd been looking—

a hint of possibility
would appear
in the form of a leaf
in midair, astray

—detached, floating,
spooling, falling—

an autumn glimmer
that catches the eye,
living the moment
of a shooting star.

Our star.

# Alone, by a Window, Waiting

Adrift in a hover-world
high overhead,
snowflakes stall
in a street lamp's halo,
singled out seemingly
entirely by chance

to transform freely
in the setting at hand
into wisps of bright light
—climbing, soaring,
drifting, posing—
thoroughly the wind's
obedient creature

even on a journey
of untold surrenders,
alone in the presence
of a fate foretold,
where no part of waiting
is more like it is
before the telling happens.

# On a Canyon Ridge

He sings in the ear of the speechless child,
who may not know if a song is a person
or a person is a song.

She extends her hand through misty air,
maybe to find where a song comes from
or where a song may go.

Who knows what this child knows,
eyelids braving a steady breeze, a
young tongue holding secrets in,

where she could not know the depth of despair
helplessness exacts in a father
who does not know how young-prey cope

—or how to absorb the mocking cruelty
of elusive cells raising havoc
where they hadn't thought to present before.

There is no deepening of his grasp
on learning there's nothing anyone can do
and that's all anyone does

—or on feeling her fingers groom his face,
part his cracked & peeling lips,
then close gently around his tongue,

maybe this time to hold the song,
muzzled in the grasp of silent fingers
that sing in a different way.

She wraps her arms around him tight,
stands as he stands, legs dangling,
and lets out a frantic, bellowing cry

that stops at the canyon floor.

# The Tower

How could a long-planned pilgrimage be any less moving
      in the rain?
She says this burrowed in a hotel blanket,
repeating to him what they needed to do, even in the face
      of threatening sky.

They climb the tower, quick at first, each step one step
      nearer the sky.
The scent of a summer storm arrives, followed by a steady,
      cold rain.
He wraps her in his Seaman's coat, pulled high
      to mimic a warming blanket.

Together, they hold a knitted throw, the body double
      of a crib blanket.
On tiptoes, they reach—one hand each—*up, up*
      toward the sky.
Not even sway, prominent now, coaxes them down
      from the rain.

Above, rain blankets the land below. Blanketing the rain
      is sunlit sky.

# Standing Perfectly Still on the Table

A lone bulb shines on bolts of fabric
in a kitchen that doubles as a sewing room the boy
surveys for patterns and a ruler.
A pattern, somewhere here on the table,
is fastened, he thinks, with a safety pin
from a basket the last man brought for the mother.

The first man, a young man, abandoned the mother,
who long since developed a way with fabric,
relying on instinct and patterns she'd pin
to fashion for herself, for others, and the boy
clothes she'd assemble at the kitchen table,
measured to spec with a yardstick or ruler.

A yardstick, for them, works like a ruler:
Stood on end, both transform into hemline guides
       for the mother.
Standing perfectly still on the table,
bedazzled in a gown of brocade fabric
sewn with only a temporary hem, she tells the boy
to *stick on the gown—at the 10s—*a pin.

*At the 10s*, she says. *A pin*,
she says. *Straight up, perfectly straight, the ruler*,
she says to the timid but helpful boy
to whom she's been both father and mother.
*Turn!* he says, one hand on the fabric,
and she does—one step—to his "turn" on the table.

They've done this before, set hems at the table
—her standing tall; him cautious with a pin—
for her clothes, for sure, but often to pay for cellphones or fabric.
Nothing in the room remains of the first man, except for the ruler
and the wooden yardstick the last man wields to punish the mother
and, more often now, the boy.

*Only one more! One more,* says the boy,
both hands raised from the task at the table.
*That's quite enough ...,* begins the mother,
glancing at the hem now circled in pins.
She holds in one hand a phone and the ruler
and moves with the other the light on the fabric.

(... *of this*) the mother says to herself, forearms bluer
  than the blue on the boy,
a powerful call to alter the fabric of lives played out
  at a crowded table
—where, phone held high, she aims the camera
  toward bruises she'll pin on their would-be ruler.

# Versions

We lied to each other
because we carried

baggage packed
with truths from the past,

nudged as we were
—as everyone is—

by an urge to invent
a version of self

in words that expose
the whole of ourselves

in versions to come
only later.

# Boxes of Toys

Take the space
between boxes of toys.
Space is there because
something else isn't.

Maybe this is where
time goes—in between.
The way space settles
at the edges of things,
forming shapes out of
what's not around them.

Or the way a mother
fills in for another,
relieving the hollow
where words don't happen
in settings a child
can read somehow.

Something that isn't there
could still be there.
Space, like a mother,
has a way with time.

# To Go On, Knowing

Adorned
in a coverall

of color
& gloss,

an apple
at rest

is just like us:
a core

concealed
in pliable flesh

a fall
could bruise

out of proportion,
at once,

with a jolt,
& for good.

# Memory Intact

In a glance,
she'd tell me,
a glance alone,

that I shouldn't
confess—at least
not then—to

what I'd done,
recklessly done,
pulling her in

again, once more,
to another among
the arched excuses

she'd contrive for me
when my father
was drunk.

Even now,
with her in mind, still
I tremble, memory intact,

and find in just
a drink or more, I'm in
a place I know.

# Carelessness

He turns his head
& opens an eye
to the fresh white pillow
untouched on the bed.

Only a couple of days
have passed, but
getting back
will do him good.

He plans for sure
to speak-up first
to ease those prone
to inhibition,

above all
the grieving
back-office clerk,
who lost a child
to carelessness
& lost her will to give.

For the first time since
he saw her last,
he'll have no reason
to look away
& she won't
have one either.

# Saltmarsh

If only the rain hadn't
fallen together,
provoking the coastline
to float face down,
muting the high-pitched
call of a godwit,
stranded, fragile,
wing in hand.

If somehow the saltmarsh
could heal the bird,
wading in a stand
of coastal reed,
groping, limping,
beak down to forage
for no reason other
than habit would.

If godwits in number
gather to happen,
the marsh a refrain
from a journey's risk,
stand & linger
in the balm
among them,
lift the coastline,
the marsh, the reed
& know where silence
calls from.

# Language Almost Always Means

Her good eye toggles from rays of sun
to the wedding band that carries a word
we thought would bring forever.

I lean in to whisper a tense of the phrase
she struggled to edit to fit the band
I wore at first but soon wore less,

knowing then, as we both know now,
that language almost always means
but sometimes doesn't quite.

Her eye offers mine an indifferent glance,
guides her hand to the bedside table, then
strays toward the afternoon's fading light.

I take the band she placed on the table
but do not speak a word of the phrase
that could trigger a fall in the act of telling.

Night's not the risk that the wrong word is
when self disappears in the wounds of others.
First among the powers of silence is peace.

# II

how silence settles in

# Over the Rain

In the barbed way she taunts me
by what she says
—*Go ahead. Try. Just try,*
she says—

I remember bike rides
home in the dark,
the pit of my stomach
anxious, turning

—drizzling maybe, but
clear nights too—
to find my mother
unkempt or beaten

or find she hadn't been touched
at all, her face awash
in mucus or blood
or smiling to me

when I opened the door.
Downstairs, in the kitchen,
over the rain, I hear
the back door open.

# After the Mind Comes To

A mother's key hides
in an overhead vent,
placed days ago
by a child at rest

from the all too temperamental
alchemy of chance, awaiting
whatever the mind recalls
after the mind comes to

—after the fall, after
the everyday thereafter,
the nights, the hours,
each one a torment,

the mother primed
for the child to wake,
trembling now through
buttoned sleeves, certain she hears

the child's voice—a whisper,
a whimper, a cry, a call—
over the ticks of a bedside clock,
made louder in the days

after the fall, but quieted now
by the voice she hears. *Where,*
she says. *Where is it?* she asks.
*This time.*

# Bottled Up

A mother won't ask
a father's take
on their daughter's plea
to pierce her tongue.

All of them know
what's bottled up
but none among them
is going to say.

Not one lifts a brow
from the table before them
or utters so much
as a single sound.

There's no telling how
a family evolves
to sign a language
sitting in place,

tongues tied up
under doleful eyes,
diminished by the scars
their words have left.

# What Fathers Are For

No one knows
like the mother of a child
how a child takes purchase
on the human heart,

becomes in time
someone else,
and returns in the end
the child they were

in a coming of age
as vivid & bold
as the fresh butter yellow
van Gogh spread thick
or the ultramarine
Vermeer ground pure.

Even in the role
of aging elder,
a mother adept
in the ways of knowing
is one of the things
that fathers are for.

# The Form of a Lifeform

*Look,* he said. *Look at your mother.*

This was the way my father would get
to the sense he thought he was making.
Everything about me that has to do with knowing
I knew from having looked at her.
Her face—that face—was my first form of language,
her midriff the source of the mark on my skin.
I looked at her. This was my mother, after all.
Or before all.

My mother was stupored, drugged up and snory,
unaware her robe had slipped under the sheet.
Her face was a blurred moon, puffed up and pasty,
her cheeks a cold milk-yellow. An eye was open,
rolled-over white, having turned that way
when I got her the key to get her the needle
to stick in her skin.

*Dad*, I whispered, my young head angled to tell him
—to signal—that I was the burden of my mother's sins.
My way was a matter of manner and form
that rarely told truths about her or me.
*Out in the open,* I said to my father.
(*Right here*), I whispered. (*The door left open.*)
He did not know the pass whisper.

He pulled me in with his laborer's hands
to offer the wisdom of a tribal leader.
*No one like her can tell what you think.*
This was the way with my father.

What he said about her said more about him.
*Tell me,* he said. *Just tell me who.*
Language has a way of revealing itself
in the ear of a child who has learned to listen.

We usually talked half way between us,
but this had pulled me far too near
reliable truths about me and my mother
and a beating from my furthermost next of kin.
*A man,* I said, this time not lying,
but my bowels told me don't tell him more.

Don't tell him this happens more often than he knows,
that when it does her body is bare,
and that when it is I hide in the hall
to peek in one-eyed at what she does.
From here in the hall, I am wholly overcome,
matching her breaths, some hurried, some not.

From here I can see my mother's mark,
a stain the color of red-brown wine,
born on my mother and bred onto me,
below the bone where bent hair grows
in the form of a lifeform, formed like a leaf.
Outside the wind blew upside down,
spitting in drifts a sideways rain,
accompanying the *Who?* the *Who?!* he demanded.

I looked at my mother. I saw that there is a hell
and that I will get there.

# Eyes

Before the Korean War was forgotten,
I saw the resentment on my mother's face
for the shape of the eyes renting around us.
The last time she let me—the last time I would—
I walked to my father's third floor apartment,
where the second thing he said was, *good*,
both hands gripping greasy chicken,

bloodshot eyeballs focused.
*We'll shoot at the dump then, early*, he said.
*The one by the store by your mother's house.*
*Sure*, I said like a kid is supposed to,
my stomach weak from the sight of him tearing,
the sound of him belching, the smell of tar
on his road-worker clothes.

*Won't yet stink then, early*, he said.

In the foggy morning's available light,
he paired his work boots side by side
then pulled them up & on slowly,
his thick hands skilled in the ways of means.
We left the car in an empty lot, climbed
a splintered, broken fence, and walked
toward the dump site, guns in hand.

Stalking. Not Talking.

*Shh ...*, my father whispered, watching.
He fired once and a cry shot back.
We ran to a spot where a boy lay limp,
thick blood gushing from the base of his neck.

My father said—though more to himself—
*Thank God*, he said. ("Thank God"?)
He told me to say what he'd tell me to say.

Later, at a wake where the body lay,
I kneeled by the boy, like others did.
I looked at his face, soul silent,
and a collar around where blood had gushed.
We walked from the boy, from a weeping mother,
from a facescape of people glad we did. And my father
walked when the charges were dropped.

What mattered most was the young boy's eyes.

# I Needed to Get His Attention

I needed to get his attention good.
*Don't,* I said. *She didn't,* I said
to what he said that she must have done.
No dice on either of the things I said.

I needed to get him to stop so bad
that I told him things I had invented.
*I saw,* I said. *From here!* I said.
Surely, he knew I didn't & couldn't.
Nothing I said—or said I could do—
could get the old man to stop.

I changed my tactics.
I asked him things.
*Why would she?* I asked. *A reason?* I asked for.
Nothing came back on what I asked
or on what I asked him for.

I needed to get his attention so bad
that I said what I hadn't said before.
*Snitch.*
With that, I got his attention.
He looked at me.
He dropped my mother's face.

He picked up my face.
He squeezed in hard at my ears and cheeks.
I got him to stop, right then, and speak
the first thing he said to me all day.

# A Blind Eye

The way that
*turning a blind eye*

is from what we saw
is the way I turn from

my daughter's fall.
There is a way that

*whatever you turn away from*
turns out in time to own you.

A pirouette is gradual.

# Margins

From her scalp
to the towel
on our daughter's lap
fell black hair bluer
than a dead crow mounted
on the end of a high chief's
dancing stick.

*Will I?* she asks
in what she can spare
from a tongue parched white
by the toxin she's fed.

But how can I judge
what she might get
the better of
when all there is
is the slimmest
of margins
and all there are
are odds.

# Terrified Face

I pinned him high
on the bedroom wall,
my off hand gripping
the chin of his shirt
and pounded the wall
by his terrified face,
each pound aimed
to miss just barely, each
one missing just enough.

Tonight, a front
bears down outside,
blowing in droves
a freezing rain
that strikes the house,
like it did that night,
on the window
of the room
he long since left.

# Beached on White Sheets

*After the carpet ends,* she says,
voice raised high over dueling laugh tracks,
red-end fingers pointing.
The tile—*tap, tap*—and my nerves tell me
this is where she said he would be.

Here is my father, beached on white sheets.
*My mother wants to come,* I say, getting straight
to what I wanted. Words come back
but sparely, slowly. *Straight out flat ... what I laid,*
he says. *No nails holes ... no seams.*

I do not know if he knows who I am
or if my voice can reach him.
*She does,* I say, not saying "now".
*No one laid ... like me,* he says,
holding the fingers of one hand up.

*Five hundred square ... a day,* he says.
This is my frail father now, no longer sucking
on a glass bottle teat, dead cells sucking on him.
I look through the room's decorated window,
past garland to my mother in a rented car.

*She does,* I say. *She would,* I say.
*Said 'I need more money,'* he says,
lifting himself to spit out the rest:
*'You want too much!'* he says they said.
Again I tell him what I want her to want.

*'Too much!'* ... *Too much?* my father says,
veins taut on his shaven skull, dime-sized nose holes flaring.
I look in the mirror that frames us both.
I see the red-end fingers curling, her arm pulling,
her whole body bent on coaxing me out.

I clear the car of melting snow, turn down the heat
that kept her warm, and lean toward the whirl of the coming snow,
into the wiper's swish & thump.
*How's she doing?* my mother asks.
*Better now, I think,* I say.

# A Call from the Station

*No come, no. I no say things va bene.*
        —But I'm at the station. Where you took me.

*Your Mama, she say to.*
        —Mama? No, the station you took me.

*To me.*
        —I'm back!

*You no never leave, mio cuore.*
        —Your heart, Aunt Ella? Your heart?

# Siblings

*Stop,* I say
to the secret her lips
turn rigid from
in the telling.

*Please,* I say
to a prodigal sister
our mother said
had *come out wrong.*

*Please stop!* I say,
as I once heard her say it,
with all there is
that's in me to say it

to a sister come back
for our mother's means
with tales recounting
repeated *groping*

I was too young
to grasp at the time
but not too young
to see.

I think to myself,
*what should I do?*
But how could I know
what I should do

when all we have now
is the things we say
and all we had then
was the stories we made.

# Moments Their Own

A night aide's *I can't*
to a grandmother's *Answer?*

the grandmother's *No*
to a mother's consent,

the mother's *No, please!*
to a father's hand,

the father's indifference
to a child's terror,

the child's calls
to the grandmother's room

are moments made up of moments their own,
unless the night aide finally can

or until we learn
we all should answer.

# Picture This

Picture two children
hand in hand,
seated alone
on a schoolyard bench,
giggling uncontrollably.

Now picture the bench,
green with mold,
piled in a heap
near waste containers
that store remains
of the school's old bones.

Does either remember,
does either one know,
what we saw
from our back yard
and I see now that
the leaves have fallen?

# Generations

More cagey than cheating at musical
chairs, there's something contrived
in the habit of gathering
extended family for holidays.

Beyond a reason to dread the event, few
at the table want more to be there
more than the oldest among them,
provoking the turn to contrived.

Places are set as they were last year,
but re-set with care
to reserve a seat
for the oddest among the oldest of them.

Not that the oldest are always odd.
More that the oldest have access to odd
by the day-after-day of living alone
to dull their grasp on constraint.

*No filter,* I heard my daughter say,
under her breath but no less clear
—and no more guarded than anyone speaks
when they think the target is deaf.

For us, an uncle long held the chair
till a spiteful aunt got out of hand.
Who knows how long I'll dodge their fate
with a daughter who may be on to me.

# The Calvary

From a corner in the room,
a piercing moan
awakens the ear
of infrequent guests
but neither the ear
nor the shuffling gait
of unskilled troops
who've heard this before
—time & again, heard this before—
if not from a corner,
then a table or a bed,
drowning the song
of chirping birds,
caged for the joy
of permanent guests,
who notice neither
the moan nor the song,
nor the scent that surrounds
their dwindling world,
warehoused away
from former lives,
weary children
having lost the will
to arrange for loved-ones
harder to love—or,
for that matter, needed
for love—the cavalry
having arrived in time
to manage an orderly end.

# Holiday

They hoped, at first,
that abiding love
would draw us home
for the holiday.
But failing that,
then a measure of duty,
if not —at least—
a last resort:
a debt for calls
to the ever ready
when we needed a place
to park the kids.

Nothing of this
was spoken aloud.
Nothing like this
would be.

Their table is set
for two, I'm sure
—like it was for three
when I was a child—
and will be for us
on another day
when the rueful longing
passes to us,
left to imagine
what they must know:
how silence settles in.

# Conflicted

I never laid eyes on Marc Chagall
or saw an original of his work,
but what if he painted me alive
in the way I heard his colors
are alive. *Leap off the canvas,*
I heard her say.

What I saw first, though tough to see,
I saw in the pastel room beside me
—an easel, a palette, a brush, three walls—
painted before she shaped a brow
to frame the lid on my first eye.

In time, she gave me another eye,
this one a softer shade than the first
& focused my two eyes straight ahead,
where I watched her finish a face on me
from a print of someone Chagall had painted
more to scale than she could do.

Even in a scene that brims with color,
nights are a torment, hanging here,
eyes wide open, the whites bone dry,
days made worse when the sun shines in,
light pouring over her desk & work,
the room awash in a sea of light.

*

On the walls around me are framed diplomas
& still-life copies she paints to unwind
from designing studies & awaiting data
on treatments delivered in controlled trials
to hopeful patients who'll appear as numbers
in articles published for surgeons to read.

There before the eyes she gave me, she
entered in a file double-blind data
staff recorded on a columned sheet
to show if the surgeons' treatment worked,
an act I'd seen at times before,
but this time I saw her smile at the file,
place a call, and say to the phone
—eyebrow tilted up like mine—
*I'll send the file. Won't need the sheet.*

What if Chagall *had* painted me alive,
rather than her having copied me?
I'd face the choice of facing her down,
me the passive alien observer,
her the active native actor,
who unwittingly painted a blithe witness
& has the power to close my eyes,
if not remove or disfigure me,

unless I reach for the things around me
to paint her into the scene I'm in,
her peering over the file of data,
the columned sheet in plain view,
me behind her, hands at rest, having painted
her back first.

# III

entirely alive in gesture and speech

# Written About

*No, just stop,* she says to me.

I turn from the page to listen better,
but her spirit in the pew is dreamy,
reverent, specious, & warm,
belying the carnage the stained glass shows
and the striking force of her speech & stare,
eyes obstructed by something obscure,
deepening the allusion of wistful longing,
part of my world and part of another
she whispers about as best she can:

*All forms of faith would whither
—they would— if we did not know
that we die.*

Solemn in the dark, this soul beside me
imagined a glorious rowing toward light
she now comes to think may be an illusion,
but how can I color these contradictions
in a way that would pull the distracted in?

She turns to say, *would you stop that please?*
as if there's a place where closure is.
*Either you write or you're written about,*
I say, then say, *now speak up, please!*

# In the Absence of Art

I pause in place
because I am startled
by feelings unfelt
in the absence of art.

A line break, cadence,
an echo, breath,
& the shape of the space
on the page around them
awaken in me
an interior voice,
entirely alive
in gesture & speech.

Words are a wonder
in a reader's ear,
but form tells the eye
what the ear can't see
when craft reveals
as the work unfolds
the art that's in the scene.

# What We Go By

No less than the little
we do understand,
no more than the so much
we don't understand
but, given there's more
than we're able to know,
stories are what we go by.

# Birds' Nest

This is a plan
    that stands to reason.
        Twigs and grass
            shaped & woven.

           Floors anchored
                to accommodate sway.
              Walls angled
        to hold them in.

  *Woven*
        *woven*
                *woven*
                *woven*

                just enough
            for a temporary stay,
        but how to deprive them
      the mark of possession?

      Never mind the contours
    of a family at bay. This is what
  we all would do
if function had its way with form.

# Dominion

In her presence
on the train, I am
thoroughly possessed,
powerless to abandon
my head-on stare,
hopeful like a teen hopes
to be befriended

by a boy or a girl,
a woman or a man
whose gait or style
strike envy in the teen,
ever so eager
for someone to notice
but quick to retreat
when no one does,
a victim again
of a grievous indifference
avoided only by looking away

or faced head-on
by looking closer
for a gesture, a nod, a glance
—some clue—to unlock
her sorcerous hold on me,
releasing what no one
should have on another,
the power of full dominion.

# The Penultimate Gift

I am now who she was before me:
a late mother's child, hands folded,
kneeling in an oddly awkward position,
pleading the case for life after death.

If prayer for oneself is the highest form
of conceit, who among us
doesn't hang by a thread
above what we think
is the reason to pray?
And what is that thread
but an odious cloud
that lifts in time for most of us,
but far too late for some.

We don't come & go & come back again.
*Noi non,* my mother repeatedly said.
*A turno!* she said my grandmother said.
We take our turns as living flesh
to hand to children the penultimate gift
of one last final breath.

# Next Door

A tree is dressed
in leafy limbs
that carry the weight
of the boy next door.

The boy is perched,
still & hidden, well in sight
of her bedroom window
above a dog's grim cage.

Through a child's spyglass,
the sun is a menace
to the back & neck
of the helpless dog.

Squirming at the sight
of a beam of sun,
the dog confirms
what Pavlov saw.

As calm as she appears to be,
none of her tongue-tied
facial gestures
tell why she can't
release the dog.

Or why he's never seen
her face, except in the grip
of a hidden figure, obscured
by the cover of an opaque drape.

Stand on the sidewalk. Listen
to the dog. Or watch
& find out more.

# Help

Other
than an eye
struck blind in the sun

or an ear
besieged by a nagging itch

*voice*

is the more-often
part of the body

hands
have an instinct
to help.

# Clothesline

A girl in a tank top,
hair in a bun,
looks up at a clothesline
perfectly strung
from her mother's house
to a neighbor's garage.

She offers the line just
one glance more,
then grasps the line
with her chin & hands,
the line snapping up
when she lets go,
again & again
when she lets go,

each time holding
the taut line longer,
grazing her neck
when she lets go
—burning her neck
if she hadn't before—

till she holds the line
with her chin alone,
up on her tiptoes
eyelids drawn,
her whole body tall
from ankles to neck
and struggles to keep
from letting go.

# Where the Pavement Ends

A turn, just ahead.
He's sure, just ahead
—though glare on the windshield
cautions the man.
North toward the bay,
then a sudden right
that's easy to miss,
but he hasn't yet.

After the turn,
he'll pass a bar
—and a diner, he thinks,
ahead on the left—
then by the school
where the kids will be.
He'll drive-by fast,
then ease-up slow
by the tenements
where the pavement ends

to the house where
she'll be alone inside,
just behind the door
this time,
head turned down
to absorb the blow
of what he'll say,
or have time to say,
before the kids come
barreling home.

The kids won't ask.
Still too young. But
neighbors will,
as they have before.
How'd she let this
happen again?

# Yard Sale

Unaware that I can see
from a window facing their front yard,
the couple looks—each one does—
at pieces arranged in rows on the lawn
minutes before the crowd would come.
They pause at a crib, a jacket, a duffle,
each of which has figured to them.

Tooth marks pit the drop-side crib
authorities ruled a safety hazard
well before a grandchild came.
*Wouldn't get much,* she said he said.
*Shouldn't want to,* she said back.

A rack holds the jacket he wore on trips
to arouse the attention of fascinations
I know he knew she knew about.
*Dated lapels,* she said she said,
but maybe more for me than him.

Pepper spray in a lipstick tube
stands by the duffle she bought for herself
after he sought their first estrangement.
Of this, she likely said nothing about,
although she really didn't say.

Standing alone with all they would part with,
they turn, touch, whisper, & sit,
rapt in a shorthand newly renewed,
now that neither speaks to me.

# If Even at All

Chickweed open
in morning sun
returned just now from

the scorched side of earth,
where I thought of you
and our young son

tending the garden
that I'd come home to
and you'd be recalled from,

leaving me here,
leg withered & scarred,
and him in a world he'll

reimagine, if you return
with less of yourself—or,
as he said, *If even at all.*

# Starting Over

At home, at night, our child asleep,
I ask myself, *just leave?* As if to answer
—but how could she know?—she says,
she whispers, (*God, no*).

Not even her voice is entirely her own,
darkened by the cloud she's come to inhabit
in collusion with everything
given around us.

Which of the two of us isn't flesh,
isn't the one come nearly undone?
Starting over is worse at night.
Too easy to just give in.

# Another Day

I remember now
I forgot to say
I'm sorry to call
so late.
Orders were strong.
I did say that.
Weren't last year,
but were today.
Enough to cover
the month, I said.

But I didn't say
who I saw out here.
Out here at a show,
of all places.

I didn't say
I heard a lot.
Or that the years
were good to her.
I save for myself
what I heard from her
and what the years
had spared her from.
And didn't say,
given the time, I'd
be another day.

# Tonight

Storms collide
in a deafening rant,

foretelling the quarrel
a couple awaits.

Rough weather,
weathered love.

# The Lead

What if I tell my wife I'm leaving
to *pick up something the doctor said*

but keep from her, if only for now,
my plan to drive over fallen leaves,

raked to the road for the town to take,
under which—if things go right—

something may well be. Not that something
ought to be, more that something may be.

What would the chance of that be
—of something breathing under the leaves?

Has to be less than finding a needle,
since leaves are piled all over town,

not in a stack like a needle would be.
How could I be blamed for that,

driving where nothing alive should be?
That should work, "… the doctor said."

But don't tell my wife. I'll tell for sure
—if this one puts me in the lead!

# Deception

When a chill arrives
in the wake of news
she'd violated a public trust

—despite her claim,
*I didn't, wouldn't!*
belying the calls
of innocent others,
who'll say they knew
or they could tell—

she'll know, or should,
when she looks at me,
she'll want to look just right.

# Why Do We Lose Our Sense of Proportion?

In school, it simply wasn't safe
to let kids know the work made sense.
You wouldn't get beaten or bullied so much,
but you would get puzzled, threatening looks.
I hid from kids that I liked to read,
understood the math we did,
and considered a highlight
of each school year

a trip to the philharmonic. In the year
that math took a startling turn
—from numbers alone to letters too—
I thought that kids were catching on.
Rather than plan a science project
teachers knew that I could do,
I plotted a scheme to head kids off.

I removed the face of an old gear-clock
that hung on our landlord's cellar wall,
clamped the gears to a project board,
and wrote at the top in magic marker,
"The Internal Workings of a Clock."

That was it. Nothing more.
The school was prone to send notes home,
but that was hardly a risk for me.
My father'd long-since left the house
and my faithful but ever-distracted mother
—hands on beads, if not in the sink—
was busy tending to neighbors in need
when a note from a puzzled teacher came.

I got the grade I knew would work,
secured my secret from the kids,
and brought to an irreversible end
my grade-school teachers' faith in me.
Why do we lose our sense of proportion
in the face of a risk we overthink,
only to find that the risk in view
isn't the one we face?

# From Inside the Jewelry Store Window

*I can't,* I said. *Please,* I said.
*I can't,* I said to what he said to do.
*Take it,* he said. *No,* I said.
*It's yours,* he said. *No,* I said back.
He stomped the floor with the heel of his boot.
*This is your chance to get it,* he said.
*Take it,* he said. *Reach in!*

I reached—I did—but knew I couldn't
in the way I can when
no one's looking.
*I can't,* I said.
He pulled back the curtain.
*Who do you know*
*don't take what's his?*

He dropped the curtain.
He picked up my face.
He looked in my eyes, up close & in.
*This is the kind of kid I got?*
*I can't,* I said. *It's yours!* he said.
*I can't right now.*
They looked at each other, then at me.

*'Gotta pee.* I said. *Pee?* he asked.
*At a robbery?* his girlfriend said.
*Ain't robbery,* he said.
*I 'gotta, I do!* I said.
I looked at my father.
He couldn't have been more stunned & still.
Not in my mother's store, he couldn't.

# Isn't It Better That She Knows?

Me? You think you're kidding me? Hey, this is David. Remember me? I'm the guy who first fell for your diversions. I'm the guy you kept from telling what *you* showed me. What *you showed me!*

And little did I know what you'd show anybody, including what you let fall out in front of my father—yeah, that's right, *my* father—before conniving him out of whatever it was you were conniving him out of. The man you *called* father, for God's sake!

This isn't about your hand. Like hell it is! This is about your chance to claim your fortune—with the same hand, no less, you used to endorse the checks I sent for what you called matters of life or death. "I can't say for what. I can't tell you why."

I'll tell you why you can't say for what! Look, you meant little to me in childhood, less later, and nothing now in middle age. Do you hear me? Nothing! I don't want to see you. I don't want to know you. I don't want to know anything about you. Are you listening to me?

Are you listening to me tell you that in the years since you last saw fit to call me, I've not spent even so much as one minute of my time thinking about you fondly. *Fondly,* I said. Did you hear me say "fondly"? Which is to say, I haven't thought of you *lovingly* in years!

Do you hear me? Don't you dare call me again. And don't, for God's sake, call me this pompous shit name you call me, "David". Never the name your mother called me. Oh, no. Never the name of *anybody* that might divert attention from your view of what others might view as the importance of the person named.

Robert, not Bob. Charles, not Charlie, even though no one called Charles Petteruti anything other than Charlie, except for the people who called him names. And speaking of names, I'll tell you the name!

# IV

a word is especially good to have

## To Stand for Them All

Words are because
we need a way
so everyone else
will know.

So why no word
for the ups & downs
when a needle biopsy
has nothing to tell?
Tension, bliss,
& the apathy after
could use a word
to stand for them all.

You can't say, *Phew!*
and say no more.
Colloquial expressions
go to the word
but don't quite make
a satisfying case
for a reason to go
no further. Not with all
the functional space
in cells absolved
for now. A word

is especially good
to have for something
you'd rather not
have to say.

# Breeze

A hot summer Sunday,
a sliver of a breeze.

She battles but succumbs
to a sordid urge
to lift her blouse
to the sun, to the west,
to the tall boy startled
by what she's done.

She knows he can see her,
knows at once, but
there is no way to stop this now.
The urge I mean.

# If Only She Hadn't Opened the Door

He files her face
with the prints

of his fingers,
retouching makeup

his hands unmade.
No one can witness

an act unhappen.
All she did was open

the door, exposing
what's best left kept secret.

Here on the floor,
she is oddly misshapen,

a planting from the garden
they tended poorly

in a scene contrived
to alter truth

now that their secrets
are almost the same.

# Escalation

Say *yuck,* his sister Lynn would say,
egging-on her friend, Anh,
skin as pure as the fallen snow,
her house the envy of his young eyes
when the door shut tight behind her.

*Yuck,* she'd say—then Anh would say—
again & again, Anh would say,
whispered maybe, but straight at him,

over & over, just that word
spoken at almost every turn,
almost the only word he heard
out loud from her—from them, toward him—
until he got them good.

# Attitude

Often the toughest
day of the year,
the day after Christmas,
a Monday this year,
is a day my turn
on a two-person shift
will be to lift & haul.

*All that trash,* I told
my partner,
who knows I owe her
—at least this year—
as she owed me
our first year on,
when the only day
I called-in sick
was a day it was
my turn to drive.

As long as I've
put-up with the cold,
I sense a change
in climate now, even
on less forgiving
days. As far as it goes,
anyhow.

# What Have They Told You?

I awaken to tubes, a curtain, a light,
& the droning rant of game-show applause.
Smiling, my mother presses a button.
*We should have before,* my mother says.
*Come in before,* she tells me. I look straight
into my mother's eyes & make the conversion
frame-by-frame, like a slow-motion camera,
from the confident eyes that mothered me then
to the angst her brow reveals now.

A doctor, a nurse, or a therapist enters
to probe gently at my neck & chest
then hard & deep at my stomach & groin.
My bowels tighten but I hold my own.

The hand whisks hair from lips that whisper,
*what have they told you? Told you before.*
She asks me this, part probing, part knowing.
I don't say lumps have formed in my lungs
or my time left if timed right is months. I don't
say what's failed, what's failing, what's feigned;
who's passed on, who's left still, who's gone.
I instead tell a tale spun tall around lies
to keep from my mother what everyone knows.

# The Roofer

Up the ladder, down the ladder,
shingles, hammer, nails in tow,
the hardwood roofer
waits all day
for the coming night,
releasing him
to shape the fabric
he sews alone at home.

He's making a shirt,
a checkered plaid,
in what he imagines
would be the size
to fit the boy
his ex has got
but yearns to raise himself
unjudged.

For years, he's worn
the clothes he's sewn,
though always
under the clothes he bought
and over the secret
he hadn't shared
with anyone other
than who she told.

Roofing pays the bills for now,
but sewing's been
his soulful balm,
the riddle he won't let on about,

though surely some
could grasp his hope
to raise a son free to be
who he longs to be himself.

# When You're Alone

So liberating
when the mind wanders.

The face erases
all sign of phrasing.
Nothing on the body
puts on airs. No
pretense, tactics,
pose, or ploy

and all that awaits
is suspended in time.

These are the moments
guarded demeanors
relax to dissolve
the sin of pride.
A blessing this happens
if it happens enough.

Real life is when
you're alone.

# Out of Reach

An older guy
—paid more, I'm sure—
works the same job I do,
spinning molds in a casting shop
that roughs-out costume jewelry.

Day after day, I haul lead fragments,
enough for our two casting pots
that melt the lead into molten broth
we mold into trinkets & rings.

Barrels of lead are one floor up,
where quiet women
in magnified glasses
sit in a hunch over spun-cool molds
to break the rough, coarse treasures free,
exposing spines of by-product lead
they toss in barrels to melt again.

*Thanks,* he says. Always says.
But all I did was belittle him,
having placed the lead
just out of his reach,
inviting him to wave me closer,
an excuse to unleash my waiting rage
for crossing a line the women see.

# Their Version

The wife leans in to tell me the worst part.
*The footsteps! So creepy. You don't think. You run.*
Her hand holds a nightgown high on her neck.
The husband says, *you run!*
There's bare leg below the hem of his coat.
*Right over here,* I think he says.
The healthy side of his shaven face
has no more expression than the palsied side.

I drop my bag at the foot of the bed.
*Took a picture?* I ask.
*Had it when he ran,* she says.
*He ran?* I ask.
His fingers tap a zoom-lens camera.
Hers cling to her nightgown top.
*Saw nothing?* I ask.

*Well, there was a car,* my wife says.
The husband & wife look at my wife.
Then they look at me.
*Yes,* they say, almost together.
*You saw it?* I ask.
*Heard it,* she says.

*Description?* I ask. *Of what?* my wife asks.
*What you heard.*
*A muffler,* she says.
*Before they got here?* I ask my wife.
*Of course,* she says. *Then you came in.*

There's rouge on her cheeks, liner on her lids,
and her lips are painted to match the lids.
*Cancelled?* she asks.

101

*Delayed,* I say. *Connection left.*
I look at them close. All three of them close.
If I didn't know his face had fallen,
I'd say their faces all looked the same.

# Tablescape

It is, I tell you, for God sake, a curse,
this arranging I do to square things off
to right them with the sides of table tops:
proofs, pencils, drafts, drives, disks, galleys,
notepads, ink. Look—look!—even as I say them,
look how I order them, rightly uttered from front to back.

Oh, it's so hard to show you & tell you too,
when what it is is what I do when my fingers stop typing:
fingertip denial of tabletop thumps. Side to side, each a bit louder,
one side of the middle one to the other side of the middle one,
each getting less than the other one got,
the loudness earned by fewer thumps,

the middle one deprived of even one.
The middle one gets none? Doggone right
the middle one gets none.
The middle one works alone. The middle one works
when I figure someone who has messed with my rights to order
gets what they got coming. Someone, anyone, including the one
who fooled with my volume.

*We'll need to drop a signature,* she said.
*Drop a signature?* I said.
*There's not enough at the end,* she said.
*Drop that, you drop a chapter,* I said.
*Yes,* she said.
*No,* I said. *There'd be nineteen!* I said. *So?* she said.
*Oh, no!* I said back.

Eighteen, maybe. Okay on eighteen, maybe. But nineteen?
She circled her chin with an index finger,
then signed her name to what looked like it mattered.
The next thing she did, she said, *Mm hmm,*
& looked up to say, *I'll tell you what. My doing this
doesn't mean we can't.*
Can't?

She raked her hair back. I thumped.
*Thump, thump, thump, thump, thump.*
*Thump, thump, thump, thump.*
*Thump, thump, thump.*
*Thump, thump.*
*Thump.*

Thump?

Good God, all of my fingers were working together!
I tell you, every one of the ones I got was working like
they were one.
The middle one was not working alone.
Oh, no. No need here for the middle one to work alone.
Not here. Not with her. Not with her looking at me
& me looking back.

Not with her smiling at me & me smiling back.
I tell you, this was an epiphany. A damn lifesaver
if there ever was one!
Damn the signature.
Right there, I tell you.
Right there on the table.

Right there in her office on top of the table were things that to me
were badly out of order: lips, a kiss, a scar, toe pads.
*Could you move just a bit to the side?* I asked.
*What?*
*A bit to the side if you would?* I asked.
*To the side?* she said.

*Yeah,* I said back.
*Here?* she said.
*That's too far to the side,* I said. *Would you mind just maybe
a little bit back?*
Damn & damn & damn & damn.
She wasn't getting it right.
She wasn't getting my rights right under any authority you care
to summon:

a book on manner, a totem, a creed, Nana signing a nighttime song.
Look—look!—there it is again. The curse? Yes!
But so much more. The things I can tell you
that haven't been said.
The things I arrange on the tables I thump.
The things I can tell you that now I can shout!
My God! Do you see it?

Freedom!

# The Getaway

First, we were all prepositions,
articles, & nouns: *At a crossroad.*
*Of a mind? On to the drawbridge. On!*

We paused until the drawbridge opened,
but then the choice of an action verb:
*Stay? Go? Run?*

Then we strung some gerunds out
—*thinking, choosing, driving* away—
all in the name of an anagram that said
not *yes,* but *no!*

*Stay? No! Thinking of driving,*
*but choosing at 'GO' to run!*

They'll pay no mind, surely not,
not to the crossroad & not to the bridge.
Not unless their parts of speech
play out for them like ours did.

# A Forties Film Noir Double-Cross

I may be wrong on what this is.
Say I plan to *hold out.*
Not a hold *up,* mind you. Hold *out.*
On you, let's say.
Oh, there is a kind of holding out
on what you might expect of me,
like Cairo offering Spade five grand
for a lavishly-jeweled onyx bird.

That's holding *out,* for sure, since
the bird's worth so much more!
Not that I'm holding *out* on you. Just yet.
A little too early to play that hand.
Too much risk you'll see what's coming.

I'll bide my time.
It's *needing to* I'm waiting on.
*Needing to*'s on hold for now.
Needing to hold *out,* that is.
*Up* I'm doing; you just don't know it.
*Out* is a film noir double-cross,
like Cairo tried on Sam Spade.
I want both an *up* and *out*
to get what I've got coming.

# Scrimshaw

All you need for
scrimshaw
is a knife and a whale
—or a walrus
if the whale swims
too far from shore—
and a lie to tell
in lyric or verse
through a veil of ink
in interlocking lines

that enchant collectors'
sense for the sublime
but insult a native's
reverence for the whale,
incarnate with species
perished in vain,
demanding she belie
what the scrimshaw claims
in a voice that trembles
in furious conviction,

insisting the whalers
be made to confess
what the scrimshaw reveals
they did at will,
likely at dusk
and far enough at sea
to mask the slaughter
of a life-giving whale
that could only be felt
in a human way

if the line art is read
by a knowing elder
—or a shadowy figure
on the far side of rain—
aghast at the carnage
adrift near shore
and able to interpret
for collectors to hear
what scrimshaw leaves
unsaid.

# Why Her Neighbor Took His Life

Death
isn't the threat

that scandal
is.

# Treasure

Alone
in the midst
of untold numbers
sleeps unfed
in a makeshift tent
one child more
than the world
imagines, one more
less to be.

# Calling

Our stone is warm
in late-day sun
earth turns
the stone
away from

& toward
the chill
of another night
calling to you
in the half empty
grave.

# Sisters

They have no reason
to visit this grave,

except
for the things
they left behind:

a surname carried
from a town overseas,

small eyes
a thin black liner
forgives,

patience for the ways
of callous men,

each other,
themselves,
him, him

and a winter chill
grown children know.

# Afterlife

Could it be
in the end,
or near the end,

that pursuit
in life
of an afterlife

is pursued
on earth
by the dead
already?

Isn't life
supposed
to be?

# After

Her glow belies
a dark horizon,
where hills resist
a falling sun
she said, *wouldn't
set* without her.

I don't know why
I'm drawn to sunlight
framed in windows
facing west
or why the shadow
darkness forms
shades my hand
but not her face.

Did dust I saw
in beams of light
know my eyes
would follow them
and she'd be gone,
all at once,
just before
the sun had set?

I sit & stare
at the darkened window,
obsessed with what
she also said.
*If less would only
happen more,
after wouldn't
have to.*

# The Artist's Palette

Even in black & white, the colors

*red, orange, yellow, blue*

merge on the palette & bleed in between,
each one free to mingle in the mind,
a smorgasbord of maddening disorder

till the artist returns to the waiting easel
in an angling, ambling assembly of motion
to transform the canvas into lines & shapes
that arrange color as the colors would be,

leveraging the palette's elusive guile,
openly alive in the artist's absence
when the palette doubles as a restful berth
for the colors to think out loud.

# V

the alter ego of making do

# Fate

1.

We acknowledged Adam's changing look
through eye talk, nods, & silent glances
until the night Kay found her nerve.
*They'd help him now, I think,* she said,
*if tests they got could tell.*

My appetite stalled—and stalled again
in the hours after tests were done,
awaiting results but dreading calls,
ignoring the signs in Adam's eyes:
crossed, heavy, red-end lids,
mucus mounded on curly lashes
Kay once called, *a woman's dream.*

The doctor told us, *Down. Mosaic.*
*Not severe, not profound.*
The words were largely new to us,
but came alive sometime later
when I saw a boy in a fast-food line,
up on his toes, hands bent at the wrist,
lips struggling to spit-out a word
in the shadow of his mother's quiet calm
& the smile that masked my face.

Soon Kay folded inside of herself,
into the abyss I'd been resisting,
returning at times to say odd things
like, *should we tell him? Does he know?*
Kay became a third-person reference
in my & Adam's first-person world.

Why is that so often the way
for the one you hope to lean on?

2.

Adam was with me all I could
—nights, weekends, the odd day off.
But he wasn't one day weeks later
when he had a spell of high-speed rage
& low-pitched grunting
neighbors heard through open windows
Kay kept closed to keep things in.
He slammed doors, chanted, grunted,
jumped, darted, stooped, screamed,
terrifying Kay when he reached for her
& surprising me when I walked in.

What could I do to calm my boy,
pants unbuttoned & riding low,
transformed at dusk like a werewolf would?

*It happens. It has. It does,* Kay said.
*You've seen this, then?*
She nodded, yes.
*But this is more when he's seen me.*
I could have told the doctor more.
Instead, I asked, *can Down do that?*

*Could, yes,* the doctor said.
*But could just be blood sugar too.*
*What does he see?* the doctor asked.
*Between you two at home,* she said.

120

Kay looked down. She didn't speak.
*You're patient with him?* the doctor asked.
*Much as we can,* I said back.
Kay didn't look at her or me.

The doctor filed her naked lip,
then said, *I know. Now listen to me.*
She said we needed qualified help,
but not the kind that visits the house.
She recommended a state-run place
—a "home" she called it, like others did—
that black-shawled matrons years ago
mocked in arabesques of gesture
to punctuate their old world speech.
*Abbandono,* I heard them say.
Abandoned, shuttered, left to fend.

I said, *No, I'll care for him.*
We talked skilled care & public aid
—the doctor about it, me around it—
then the doctor pulled me in.
*You're raising a child you can't alone.*
I knew she knew things closed to me,
but I didn't expect that she'd deliver
the clarifying moment of my son's life.

Driving back from admitting Adam,
I felt like I think it feels to drown.
Once you give up, it's a relief.

3.

Kay's pregnancy caused some scares:
cysts, fatigue, & a thyroid problem
that explained the weight she piled on
& the spotting that sent her straight to bed.
She carried on with little fuss,
humbling me to realize
that mothers almost everywhere
do things children never see.

*Nine out of ten on the Apgar,* Kay said,
a newborn body nestled in her arms,
the browns of his eyes bright & knowing.

All we saw was clement weather.

4.

The home presented like a place forbidden,
even in a well-staged front façade:
weather-beaten walls, worn-down steps,
& thick imposing double doors
stranded behind tarnished gates.
By a miracle of engineering,
the doors & gate, heavy as they are,
open almost effortlessly.

The ground floor holds a row of offices,
one-by-one down a cavernous hall.
Globe lights hang from chrome pipes,
each outside a windowed door

that spells-out what goes on in there:
STAFF, LAUNDRY, PERSONNEL.
Most say how they run the place.
None say how they help the kids.

I gave a name & a voice came back,
*2-1-2, one floor up. Left side,*
*past the attendants' station.*

Adam was alone, shirt unbuttoned,
rocking on the legs of an upright chair,
a whiff of something when he rocked back,
masked a little when he leaned in.
They'd cut his hair off pretty much
—a "baldy sour," we said as kids—
exposing the shape of a trapezoid,
suggesting to me, for the first time really,
that something's missing, not something's wrong.
His pants—someone else's pants?—
seemed to me too short, too,
the cuffs high over scruffy shoes,
the crotch soiled from who knows what.

He looked like someone else to me:
The younger face
of the father I've seen
in photos he'd not been cut from.

Leaning in, I talked to him
but knew that there was no one there,
focused, it seemed, on something, I guess,
but likely, I think, on nothing I know.
Sitting on the bed, but still talking,
I looked in close at his shaven head

& then in the mirror facing me
—at lines on my face
arranged in the shape of matching brackets,
at dashes around eyes made small
by aging lids, at cuts on my cheek
from an errant saw forming the slope
of misplaced commas.

Clues that speak to a person's past
punctuate their face.

5.

Kay was awake when I got back
from a job I got a day away.
My being gone meant Kay was alone
& meant she might have something to say.

*A man supports you. You let him,* she said.
*You make a life with the kids,* she said.

What do you say to a thing like that?
*What do you want from me, Kay?*
The veins in her forehead bulged blue.
*A lot of things, I want,* she said,
*like my own house, no one else upstairs,*
*and a kid that walks and claps his hands!*

*You married me for what?* I asked.
*No one marries for a reason why,* she said.
*You marry when it's time. To what's there then.*

We didn't talk in the coming days,
or the day she felt the time had come
to go by bus to see him.
I found her there when I walked in,
unconsciously chewing her bottom lip,
eyes turned toward, but not quite on,
the one exposed low-watt bulb
that kept the coming dark at bay.

There she was & there she wasn't.
The alter ego of making do.

6.

I picked him up for a birthday, his,
& just for the afternoon, but still.
*See he eats,* the attendant said,
under the umbrella he held for us.

Adam lost all sign of calm
—furrowed brow, grinding teeth—
as we drove by places he would have known:
Lido's Beach, where he'd wade for hours
in little more than an inch of surf. Crescent Park,
where he'd board a train in Peanut Land
on kiddy rides beneath his age.
Calm returned with the sound of tires
on the gravel beside our tenement.
I released the buckle that held him in,
& let him push my hand away.

Kay appeared, fully dressed,
from her now near-constant bedroom exile.
She'd decorated as best she could
—a "Happy Birthday" table cloth
& two standing number candles
that added-up to about his age.

Adam stomped on the outdoor mat,
then scraped his shoes on an indoor throw.
*Shut the door!* Kay said to me
in a voice that seemed to pierce the air.
There was something in the way he looked at her.
And the way he looked at me.

Still on his feet, stomping briskly,
he impounded all his weight & fury
into a backward flying fist
that snapped Kay's head
like a close-up shot
of a half-dazed fighter.
He seemed to possess the dizzying power
at the intersect
of relieving an itch
& dealing a bare-hand beating.

7.

*Don't quite know what comes of this,*
the home's director said to me,
before he said, in his opinion, Adam
*won't be released* to me,
not if Kay *presses charges*
for what she says I did.
Charges?

He looked at me with a smug grin
that served to renew
his hold over me.

Turned away from Adam & Kay
—surely for now, if not for good—

I rose from a chair set lower than his
& left without a word,
oddly content in the newfound freedom
walking-away endowed in me, alone
now with the things I'm scared of
—& the accidental chemistry of fate.

# What Strange Things Lurk

*after A. Wilber Stevens*

The sum of my things is packed in boxes
stacked in a hall by a room I rent.
*Move it,* the landlord says again
and certainly said to others before

with hardly a hint of opposition
from tongues beat back into silent glances
on hardened people who don't talk back,
even in the face of more to come.

What strange things lurk high overhead,
threatening to cast a revealing light
on a past that had no future. Is staying
the course an undertaking for heroes

or a stop on the path to the still empty grave?

# About the Author

Born in Rhode Island, David Ricchiute lives in Indiana. Poetry and fiction appear or are forthcoming in *NOON*, *POEM*, *Tampa Review*, *North Atlantic Review*, *Interim*, *First Intensity*, *Red Rock Review*, *American Journal of Poetry,* and *Tipton Poetry Journal*, among others. Formerly the Deloitte Professor of Accountancy, University of Notre Dame, he is the author of *Auditing* (Cengage) and research on judgment & decision making in the *Journal of Applied Psychology, Journal of Experimental Psychology, Journal of Accounting Research,* and *Organizational Behavior & Human Decision Processes.* He is a volunteer at the South Bend Beacon Children's Hospital Ronald McDonald House and at the Northern Indiana Center for Hospice Care.

33610638R00078